BIBLE 1210
THE CHRIST

CONTENTS

Author: **Barry G. Burrus, M.Div, M.A., B.S.**

Editor: Alan Christopherson, M.S.

Illustrations: Melissa Evers

Kyle R. Bennett, A.S.

Alpha Omega Graphics

Alpha Omega Publications ®

804 North 2nd Avenue East, Rock Rapids, Iowa 51246-1759
© MM by Alpha Omega Publications, Inc. All rights reserved.
LIFEPAC is a registered trademark of Alpha Omega Publications, Inc.

THE CHRISTIAN

Although we often acquire our beliefs from other people, especially our parents, we must make them our own by the conviction of the Scriptures through the Holy Spirit.

In this LIFEPAC®, the Scriptures, God's nature and the basic truth claims of Christianity will be studied, for a clear understanding of these increases apologetic skills. Christian growth and how we mature will also be studied, as will how the Christian affects those they have contact with. Through teaching, we are called to defend the faith against cultic beliefs or heresies. Each life we touch, in turn, touches others.

OBJECTIVES

Read these objectives. The objectives tell you what you will be able to do when you have successfully completed this LIFEPAC.

When you have finished this LIFEPAC, you should be able to:

1. Discuss the Trinity.
2. Explain the meanings of Christ's redemptive work and justification by faith.
3. Tell the importance of the Biblical canon.
4. Describe the work of the Holy Spirit.
5. Identify the fundamental differences between cults and Christianity.
6. List activities that contribute to spiritual development.
7. Explain the truths upon which Christian conduct is based.
8. Identify the influences on vocational and ministry choices.
9. Explain the importance of proclaiming the Gospel.

Survey the LIFEPAC. Ask yourself some questions about this study. Write your questions here.

_____
_____
_____
_____
_____
_____
_____
_____
_____
_____

I. WE BELIEVE

Scriptural doctrine is the basis of Christianity. The vanguard against error is discernment brought through study.

Our faith begins with the Trinity. Our sole authoritative source of information about the person of God is His written record, the Bible. The Bible is the whole counsel of God concerning all things necessary for His glory, man's salvation, faith, and life. In this section, you will see how God dwelt with the nation of Israel, and how in these last days, He gives grace to all nations through Christ. The Spirit of God enables believers to discern the truth and defend it.

SECTION OBJECTIVES

Review these objectives. When you have completed this section, you should be able to:

1. Discuss the Trinity.
2. Explain the meanings of Christ's redemptive work and justification by faith.
3. Tell the importance of the Biblical canon.
4. Describe the work of the Holy Spirit.
5. Identify fundamental differences between cults and Christianity.

VOCABULARY

Study these words to enhance your learning success in this section.

canon

condescension

herald

linguistics

metaphysical

polytheism

scribes

 Read John 1, 2 Corinthians 13:14, and Isaiah 48:16.

THE NATURE OF GOD

The Trinity is the single most important doctrine in Christianity. It is the linchpin upon which stands Christ's Atonement, His Incarnation, and ultimately, our Salvation.

The Trinity. Our only source of primary knowledge of the Trinity (Father, Son, and Holy Spirit) is the **canon** of Holy Scripture. The emphasis of the Old Testament was on the revelation of God as YHWH (I AM, Yahweh), the one and only God, contrasted with the **polytheism** of all other nations. The Israelites used what we call the Old Testament as their source of authority on personal and religious conduct.

God dwelt in the presence of (yet separate from) His holy nation, Israel. He abode between the cherubim on the Mercy Seat (the gold cover on the Ark of the Covenant) (Exodus 25:22). The Ark was kept in the Holy of Holies to be seen only once a year, on the Day of Atonement, by a single high priest. During the wilderness wanderings, the Ark was carried in front of the people.

His presence continued with them until His wrath was finally kindled at Shiloh (Psalm 78:60). The Israelites followed other gods once again, thereby breaking their covenant with God, and He withdrew from them. He delivered them into the hands of their enemies at Ebenezar. The sons of Eli took the Ark of the Covenant into battle, thinking it would save them. Israel was defeated by the Philistines and the Ark was captured.

✒ Complete these sentences.

1.1   The three Persons of the Trinity are the a. _____ , b. _____ , and c. _____ .

1.2   Israelites used the Old Testament as their authority in a. _____ and b. _____ conduct.

1.3   God withdrew His physical presence from Israel because _____ _____ .

1.4   Israel was defeated by the a. _____ , and the b. _____ was captured.

After God's "physical" presence departed from Israel, He ministered to them through kings, prophets, and the Law. Although allusions to multiple Persons within the Godhead are made, the Hebrew Bible is clear in its monotheism. He was called El or Elohim and YHWH (I AM). (See LIFEPAC 1204, Section I)

God's names YHWH, Elohim, and Adonai were all later used to refer to Jesus, the Messiah. Jesus claimed, "Verily, verily, I say unto you before Abraham was, I AM" (John 8:58).

Jesus Christ, the Word of God, is God. "In the beginning was the Word, and the Word was with God, and the Word was God. The same was in the beginning with God. All things were made by him; and without him was not any thing made that was made" (John 1:1-3). God the Holy Spirit was also active in Creation, for "In the beginning God created the heaven and the earth… And the Spirit of God moved upon the face of the waters" (Genesis 1:1,2b).

God's personal name is YHWH (Exodus 6:3). In this name, He proclaims that He (I AM) is the self-existent one not depending on anything to sustain Him. To the Jews, he proclaimed Himself as fully righteous. He called His people to be set apart (as He is) in righteousness among the nations, being in effect His **heralds** on the earth. Being Creator, He is involved and sovereign over all He created, while the pagan gods were only wood and stone.

When God the Son came to earth, He revealed to us God's trinitarian nature. We see what the Father is like through Christ himself, for He came to fulfill God's law in the flesh, and pay the price for the sins of all His redeemed. Before the foundation of the earth, the Trinity knew that Jesus would have to pay the price to save us from our sin. God's holiness cannot allow sin in His glorified presence. Therefore, Christ's righteousness alone gives us access to God, for any other way but Him brings Judgement.

God, the Holy Spirit led national Israel through the wilderness and into Canaan. He leads us to Christ and enacts our salvation. He blesses us with wisdom and discernment.

✒ Complete these activities.

1.5   On a separate piece of paper, answer the following questions in one or two paragraphs. You may use any source or person to help you.

    a. What is your value to God?

    b. Where does salvation come from?

    c. What is the work of the Holy Spirit?

✓ Adult check   _____
                             Initial   Date

Read Hebrews 1 and Acts 1.

Holiness. The Trinity is *holy*, meaning *separate* or *sanctified*. Yahweh created all things, yet is separate from His creation. He cannot be correctly compared to any created thing. Only through an act of His mercy did He allow us to understand His nature. The mercy was in His Son, Jesus. God explained His trinitarian nature in the best way man could understand. The Trinity is clearly fact, but to us it is a holy mystery. The Son desires to be subject to the Father to the point that He came to earth and physically dwelled with us in the midst of our sins and despair. Only in His **condescension** to humanity would man be saved.

Throughout Scripture, God is declared as being holy. In Leviticus the words, "I am holy" are frequently repeated (Leviticus 11:44-45, 19:2, 20:26, 21:8). When the Holy One of Israel made a covenant with David, He proclaimed the holiness of the coming Messiah.

At the beginning of His ministry, Christ's followers did not realize He was the Holy One of God, but His identity was clearly known to evil spirits (Mark 1:24). Peter lived in the presence of God's holiness, but it took God, the Holy Spirit to reveal His true identity to him. Not until after His sacrifice did His disciples fully realize His deity.

Although Christ taught His disciples many things after His Resurrection, they were still not equipped to be His witnesses. Before His Ascension, Jesus explained that He would not leave them alone. He promised to send God the Holy Spirit, who would reveal the meaning of all the teachings He had given them. He equipped them to perform the works that Christ performed and to even do greater works than He did (John 14:12-26).

The Spirit of God regenerates our soul, which is dead in sin. We immediately trust (have faith) in Christ's sacrifice to atone for our sins. The Holy Spirit is our seal for eternity. From then on, He is our Sanctifier as He works in our hearts, continually molding us in Christ's image.

 Complete this activity.

1.6   Read Ephesians 4:23-32 and write the verse number on the line that best describes the results of the holiness of God in the believer's life.

a. _____ speaking truth

b. _____ not grieving the Holy Spirit

c. _____ working with your hands

d. _____ forgiving one another

e. _____ giving no room to Satan

f. _____ being kind

g. _____ giving to the needy

h. _____ being tenderhearted

i. _____ edifying talk that blesses believers

j. _____ quickly overcoming anger

k. _____ putting away malice

l. _____ not stealing

m. _____ not speaking evil

n. _____ not using foul language

HOLY SCRIPTURE

The Bible is the only source that reveals all things necessary for God's glory, man's salvation, faith, and life. The teaching in the local church must be in conformity with Biblical doctrine.

The vast majority of humanity does not believe that the Bible is the only primary revelation of God. However, God chose to have His communication to us reduced to the simple form of the written word. Thus, both the Old and New Testaments are authoritative and authentic testaments about Christ from God.

These books were maintained in congregations of Palestine, Asia-Minor, Greece, and Rome. They were copied and circulated among the groups of Christians, and during their dispersion, they remained intact. Some scholars believe that some early Christian writings have been "lost." Just as the Dead Sea Scrolls were found centuries after their burial, perhaps one of Paul's lost letters would be found on some occasion. However, God maintained for us the perfect record of all we need to know to be saved, live rightly, and glorify Him.

If an ancient manuscript suddenly reappeared, it is subject to certain criterion before it could be considered authoritative. For example, our Bible was quoted widely by persons who lived soon after the canon was completed. Clement of Rome wrote to the church at Corinth in the year 95 (A.D.). In his book, he quoted from Matthew, Luke, Romans, Corinthians, Hebrews, 1 Timothy, and 1 Peter. In his letter to the Philippians in 110, Polycarp quoted from both Paul and Peter's works. They were so quoted, because even then the writings were seen as Scripture.

During Diocletian's reign in the early fourth century, a final effort was made to destroy Christianity. For ten years, Bibles were burned in market places by the agents of this Roman emperor. After his death, Constantine became emperor.

Constantine ordered fifty copies of the Bible for the church at Constantinople. Eusebius (bishop and historian) supervised the copying of the existing manuscripts and delivered them to Constantinople. He then determined what books besides the Old

TRAINED *SCRIBES* CAREFULLY TRANSCRIBED COPIES BY HAND.

Testament were Scripture to believers. He differentiated them from the spurious or other heretic forgeries. The twenty-seven books accepted by the Council of Carthage (397 A.D.) are the same ones contained in the New Testament today.

Throughout history, the Scriptures have been maintained. Prior to the advent of printing, trained **scribes** carefully transcribed copies by hand. They were mindful of every jot and tittle as they labored to make exact copies.

Hundreds of translations have been completed. The New Testament was originally written in Greek, while the Old Testament was written in Hebrew and Aramaic. The Bible has been translated about twelve hundred times since the original books were written. Translations are written in order to place it in the language of local Christian groups. In 1978 scholars translated the Bible in order to yield a clearer English understanding of the authors' original intent. The result was the New International Version. Most modern versions are an attempt to put the Scriptures in a more readable form.

Archaeological research throughout the world continues to provide material and language information helpful toward understanding the Scriptures. **Linguistics** continue to expand our technical understanding of the Bible's texts.

While understanding the history of Scripture is important, nothing is more valuable than a solid knowledge of its *content*.

✏️ Complete these statements.

1.7   The two original languages of the Old Testament are a. _____ and
        b. _____ .

1.8   The original language of the New Testament was _____ .

1.9   The New International Version is a translation into the _____ language.

1.10   The Bible is the only book which reveals that which glorifies God and all that is necessary for man's _____ .

1.11   Our understanding of the language and times of the Bible writings will continue to expand through the sciences of a. _____ and b. _____ .

1.12   Manuscripts are subject to many criterion before being admitted into the _____ .

1.13   The Roman emperor who tried to destroy Christianity was _____ .

1.14   The fourth-century historian who determined which books were to be included in the New Testament was _____ .

JUSTIFICATION

In the modern church, the doctrine of salvation (the Gospel) or justification is greatly obscured by psychology and moralism. However, in order for there to be a Church *at all*, it must be clearly taught. Justification is often codified in these doctrines of grace:

1. All men are sinners and separated from God.

2. The Holy Spirit convicts His elect of their sin, gives them the new birth, and seals them unto salvation.

3. Christ's perfect life and sacrificial death fulfilled God's holy demand for the just punishment of sin.

4. All who have faith in the risen LORD Jesus' sacrifice as being for their own sin are justified.

5. The Holy Spirit feeds and maintains the faith of God's children unto the day of Judgement.

ALL MEN ARE SINNERS AND SEPARATED FROM GOD.

Before Creation, God knew that He would create man holy but that man would sin. A holy, righteous God has no fellowship with sinners. Hence, even before Creation, God planned the salvation of His creatures.

Justice dictates that all sin must be justly punished by the shedding of blood. Through the grace of our LORD, He permitted substitutionary sacrifices to remove the sin of the guilty, as practiced by the Jews until 70 A.D.

The sacrificial animals slain over hundreds of years were only a type and shadow illustrating the final sacrifice of Christ Himself on the Cross. With the death and Resurrection of God's Son, a new covenant was established with man.

Sin can never steal away a person's salvation. What God does in saving someone, man cannot undo. The plans and intentions of God can never be foiled or undone.

God chose, through His sovereign free will, to draw them to Himself (John 6:41-71). The Father and Son sent the Holy Spirit to convict us of our sin and give us the Second Birth. God teaches us of Christ. He gives us the understanding we need to comprehend the meaning of Christ's sacrifice. Our participation in the plan of salvation is to be thankful. "For by grace are ye saved through faith; and that not of yourselves: *it is* the gift of God: not of works, lest any man should boast" (Ephesians 2:8-9). "So then *it is* not of him that willeth... But of God that showeth mercy" (Romans 9:16).

Titus 3, describes the working of the Holy Spirit to bring a person to Christ. Believers are justified by the grace of God, therefore, produce good works. These good works are done out of thanks to God, a living testimony to His mercy.

Before you can deal effectively with those who are bound in false doctrine, you must have a clearunderstanding of justification. Your church or pastor's library should contain resources for you to utilize. Study these doctrines. "...(S)anctify the Lord God in your hearts: and *be* ready always to *give* an answer to every man that asketh you a reason for the hope that is in you with meekness and fear" (1 Peter 3:15).

 Do this assignment.

1.15   Write a two-page paper describing justification, including the doctrines of grace.

 Adult check   _____

                                         Initial   Date

CONTEND EARNESTLY FOR THE FAITH

Since 1900, cultic activity has dramatically increased. Astrology, clairvoyants, and mentalists are given public audiences as curiosity about them runs rampant. Satan is a reality and the earth is his kingdom. Christians need to be aware of the false doctrines of our day and to discover methods to combat these heresies.

Gnostics were **metaphysical** "super-apostles" and contemporaries of the early Christian church. The Gnostics denied Christ's Incarnation and Resurrection. They denied sin and therefore, the Atonement of Christ.

Nearly all pseudo-Christian organizations teach and produce good works, but deny Christian doctrine. Typically, they believe that there are other ways to God than by the Cross, either directly or as a result of their works.

The principle difference between Christianity and cults is in justification. Who saves who? Christianity teaches that God saves man and thus, gives access to Himself. Christianity is God-centered. The cults teach that either man saves himself (or doesn't need salvation at all) and can have direct access to God through his own desire to do so. Cults are man-centered.

Cults place a great burden on their members to produce service in exchange for upward progression or "salvation," while offering superficial solutions to today's problems. Some are renown for their welfare system or political isolationism. Others draw upon disenchanted adolescents who do not find satisfaction in materialism. All of them are seductive, but spiritually deadly.

Doctrinal errors crept into the early churches, and the Apostles spent a great deal of time refuting errors such as Gnosticism. Satan continually attempts to subvert Christians by appealing to

ALL CULTS ARE SEDUCTIVE, BUT SPIRITUALLY DEADLY.

their human weaknesses which encourage them to indulge themselves.

One of the best defenses against error and Satan is God as He indwells believers. Jesus said (John 14:23), "...If a man love me, he will keep my words: and my father will love him, and we will come unto him, and make our abode with him." The Holy Spirit of God dwells in all who have faith in Lord Jesus' sacrifice. Study diligently and the Holy Spirit will guide you away from error. To not study is to encourage Satan's seductions.

Anything contradictory to the historic truth of Scripture is a lie, for God cannot lie nor contradict Himself. Therefore, test the spirits (1 John 4:1), for many false prophets are "gone out into the world."

In a direct attack on Gnosticism, John declared that those who do not confess that Jesus came in the flesh are antichrists. He warns the church that God does not dwell in people who deny the true doctrine of Jesus. Finally, he says (2 John 10-11), "If there come any unto you, and bring not this doctrine, receive him not into *your* house, neither bid him God speed: for he that biddeth him God speed is partaker of his evil deeds."

Through study of the Word of God and dependence on the Spirit of God, we are being equipped to defend the faith against false teachings. Study cultic doctrine without subjecting yourself to the cults directly. Because of the seductive subtlety of false doctrine, you must have a rock solid understanding of the truth in order to analyze them.

 Complete this activity.

1.16   Select one Christian doctrine such as the Trinity, the Virgin Birth, the Resurrection or the Second Coming. On a separate sheet of paper, write a concise statement of that doctrine from a Christian point of view and also from the point of view of a cult. (An authoritative source for cultic doctrine is *Kingdom of the Cults* by Dr. Walter R. Martin.)

Adult check   _____
                           Initial   Date

 Answer *true* **or** *false*.

1.17   _____   The best defense against error is knowledge of cultic doctrines alone.

1.18   _____   The Holy Spirit indwells every believer.

1.19   _____   Study diligently and the Holy Spirit will guide you away from error.

1.20   _____   Various teachings, or spirits, must be tested to determine their origin.

1.21   _____   God dwells with even those who deny true doctrine.

1.22   _____   You are equipped to defend your faith through diligent study of Scripture.

Adult check   _____
                           Initial   Date

Review the material in this section in preparation for the Self Test. This Self Test will check your mastery of this particular section. The items missed on this Self Test will indicate specific areas where restudy is needed for mastery.

Put these items in chronological order. Number these in the order they were revealed to national Israel (each answer, 2 points).

1.01 ___8___ God demands righteousness.

1.02 _____ God sought individual fellowship.

1.03 _____ God was known as the Creator.

1.04 _____ YHWH was seen as the one and only God.

1.05 _____ YHWH was the God of Israel.

Match these items (each answer, 2 points).

1.06 _____ YHWH

1.07 _____ Messiah

1.08 _____ Adonai

1.09 _____ Trinity

1.010 _____ Spirit

a. great and powerful king
b. God in three persons
c. God's personal name
d. the Savior, "Anointed One"
e. the Sanctifier

Answer *true* or *false* (each answer, 1 point).

1.011 _____ Names ascribed to God were not given to Jesus.

1.012 _____ The Holy Spirit indwells non-Christians.

1.013 _____ God is a complete and equal unity of the Father, Son, and Holy Spirit.

1.014 _____ Jesus came to show us God's nature and redeem his elect from sin.

1.015 _____ The Holy Spirit dwells in church buildings just as God did in the Tabernacle.

1.016 _____ The Holy Spirit gradually conforms Christians into Christ's image.

1.017 _____ God is holy and cannot tolerate sin.

1.018 _____ All people who call themselves Christians are Christians.

1.019 _____ The Apostles knew from the moment they saw Him that Jesus was the Holy One of God.

1.020 _____ Study diligently and the Holy Spirit will guide you away from error.

Complete these statements (each answer, 3 points).

1.021 Greek is the original language of the _____ Testament.

1.022 Hebrew and Aramaic the original languages of the _____ Testament.

1.023 Bible translations are done in order to place Scripture in the native _____ of local groups.

1.024 The two sciences that can expand our knowledge of the Bible times and language are a. _____ and b. _____ .

1.025 Religious systems at odds with true Christianity are called _____ .

1.026 The Ark of the Covenant was once captured in battle by _____ .

1.027 "For by a. _____ are ye saved through b. _____ ; and that not of yourselves: it is the gift of God: not of c. _____ , lest any man should boast." (Ephesians 2:8-9)

1.028 The early historian who helped to determine the New Testament canon was _____ .

1.029   The Bible reveals everything necessary for God's a. _____ , man's
         b. _____ , c. _____ , and d. _____ .

1.030   The Roman emperor who tried to destroy Christianity was _____ .

Answer these questions (each answer, 5 points).

1.031   What does Ephesians 4:23-32 describe?
         _____
         _____

1.032   What is the primary difference between Christianity and a cult concerning salvation?
         _____
         _____

1.033   What is justification by faith?
         _____
         _____
         _____

1.034   What was Jesus' redemptive work?
         _____
         _____

1.035   What is the work of the Holy Spirit?
         _____
         _____
         _____

75 / 94

Score
Adult check _____

Initial   Date

10

II. MATURITY

Your character and spiritual maturity should be very important to you. By this time, you should be eating the meat of the Scriptures, having been weaned from the milk. As you mature, you should be able to teach others Christianity's basic doctrines. In this section you will study Christian conduct and how it is developed.

SECTION OBJECTIVES

Review these objectives. When you have completed this section, you should be able to:

4. Describe the work of the Holy Spirit.
6. List activities that contribute to spiritual development.
7. Explain the truths upon which Christian conduct is based.

SELF-AWARENESS

A great deal of psychiatry and psychology is devoted to fabricating self-esteem in people who believe their lives are pointless. Many religious cults do the same thing. Both teach that purpose is found within the individual. Mental powers are stressed, with an emphasis on self-healing or "self-resurrection."

The Christian's reason for understanding themselves is to bring glory to God. We are each unique and gifted by God with special capabilities.

Spiritual gifts. "Every good gift and every perfect gift is from above, and cometh down from the Father of lights..." (James 1:17).

The prophet Jeremiah claimed, "Thus saith the Lord... I will give them an heart to know me, that I *am* the LORD: and they shall be my people, and I will be their God: for they shall return unto me with their whole heart" (Jeremiah 24:5,7). The ability to know God is a gift. Although they suppress the truth, all unsaved men and atheists know that God exists. Regeneration, or the New Birth which ushers in Salvation is purely God's gift. Ezekiel declared that God would put within His people a new heart that is not hardened to the love of God (Ezekiel 11:19-21). This enabled you to recognize and have faith in Christ's Atonement and thus, be saved. All Christians share in the gift of salvation, and the ministry of the Holy Spirit. God gave us our individual talents in order to strengthen each other and bring glory to Him. These gifts are many, but they all come from one source, the Holy Spirit. The parable of the talents in Matthew 25, illustrates how we are to use our gifts. We are expected to use them to their greatest extent, multiplying their benefits to the world.

Some persons are talented teachers while others are good at exhortation or ministering. The gifts are many and its not possible to list them all, but whatever gift God has given to you, you must put it to use. Here are but a few:

Tender heart:	Empathy with the sufferings of others.
Organization:	Making complex arrangements with ease and efficiency.
Patience:	Calmly and orderly pursuing a goal or a complicated task.
Hospitality:	Welcoming and serving people in your home.
Love of children:	Relating to young children and their specific needs.
Praise:	Complimenting and uplifting the contributions of others.

No gift is too insignificant, and thank God for them. Support your pastor and those in visible church positions. The Apostle Paul said, "Even unto this present hour we both hunger, and thirst, and are naked, and are buffeted, and have no certain dwelling place; and labor, working with our own hands: being reviled, we bless; being persecuted, we suffer it: being defamed, we entreat: we are made as the filth of the world..." (1 Corinthians 4:11-13).

The religious freedom we have in the U.S. is not the same for our foreign missionaries. In countries where Christianity is not the major religion, persecution is often deliberate, resulting in imprisonment or death. As evil perseveres in the world, heed God's admonition: "Preach the word; be instant in season, out of season: reprove, rebuke, exhort with all longsuffering and doctrine. For the time will come when they will not endure sound doctrine; but after their own lust shall heap to themselves teachers, having itching ears; and they shall turn away *their* ears from the truth, and shall be turned unto fables. But watch thou in all things, endure afflictions, do the work of an evangelist, make full proof of thy ministry" (2 Timothy 4:2-5).

To preach Christian doctrine is to invite controversy, anger, and the wrath of Satan. He is flustered before the onslaughts of God's kingdom. The "offense of the Gospel" will follow you whenever you preach it. But be reassured, for God is sovereign and justly upholds His Word.

Choose the correct answer.

2.1 Spiritual gifts are _____ .
   a. only used by pastors and teachers
   b. usually seen in congregational worship
   c. diverse and numerous

2.2 The source of spiritual gifts is _____ .
   a. the laying on of hands
   b. the Spirit of God
   c. a Bible college education

2.3 The purpose of spiritual gifts is to _____ .
   a. multiply their benefits to the world
   b. cause a denomination to grow in membership
   c. give everyone something to do

Answer *true* or *false*.

2.4 _____ Faith is a gift of God.

2.5 _____ Christians no longer suffer for their beliefs.

2.6 _____ Because Paul was a great Apostle, he had an easy life.

2.7 _____ The LORD expects Christians to use their spiritual gifts.

2.8 _____ Spiritual gifts are to meet the needs of others and glorify God.

2.9 _____ The ability to know God is a gift from God.

2.10 _____ Only missionaries suffer because of their public ministry.

2.11 _____ Some spiritual gifts are used in full-time ministries.

Personality. We are encouraged to be gentle, forbearing, longsuffering, and meek, as Christ was. He stated, "Take my yoke upon you, and learn of me; for I am meek and lowly in heart: and ye shall find rest unto your souls" (Matthew 11:29). Christ was in subjection to His Father. Likewise, Daniel humbly relied upon God when he approached Nebuchadnezzar to interpret his dreams. Daniel bore all of the trials of his captivity in Babylon. Adversity did not stop him as he continued to interpret dreams and prophesy.

If you ever do seek the counsel of a professionally trained psychologist or counselor, choose a Christian, for Christianity's standards are not held in high esteem by secularists. For example, the Scriptures clearly indicate that a woman should be submissive to her husband. In secular counseling, women are often encouraged to defy their husbands or be unfaithful in order to produce a personality change. Secular counselors typically advise things in contradiction to Christian doctrine.

We are all self-centered by nature and even after we are redeemed it continues. Study Scripture and pray that the Holy Spirit gradually release you from your incessant self-love. The more others-centered you are, the better image of Christ you portray.

Answer *true* **or** *false*.

2.12 _____ Daniel's resolve crumbled while he was a Babylonian captive.

2.13 _____ The Scripture is unclear as to how you should behave.

2.14 _____ The Holy Spirit gradually conforms us to the character and personality of Jesus.

2.15 _____ Jesus displayed meekness and subjection to God.

2.16 _____ Secular counselors typically support Christian doctrine.

Complete this activity.

2.17 Circle fifteen personality traits from the following list that you believe characterize you. Write + beside the circled traits you consider to be desirable, and write — beside your undesirable traits. Discuss your traits with your parent or teacher.

_____ relaxed
_____ dominant
_____ emotionally stable
_____ tense
_____ childish
_____ suspicious
_____ venturesome
_____ hostile
_____ egocentric
_____ conscientious
_____ highly intelligent
_____ outgoing
_____ reserved
_____ sympathetic
_____ group-dependent
_____ uncontrolled
_____ tough-minded
_____ practical
_____ imaginative
_____ shrewd
_____ expedient
_____ trusting
_____ less intelligent

_____ timid
_____ self-assured
_____ happy-go-lucky
_____ overly affected by environment
_____ emotional
_____ sensitive
_____ nervous
_____ conservative
_____ depressed
_____ joyous
_____ selfish
_____ experimenting
_____ self-sufficient
_____ controlled
_____ peaceful
_____ apprehensive
_____ passive
_____ honest
_____ loving
_____ worried
_____ faithful
_____ tolerant
_____ obstinate

Adult check _____

Initial   **Date**

Temptation. Job pleased God. God knew Job could not be turned away from his faithfulness, and He allowed Satan to test him in very distressing ways. He first allowed Satan to destroy his family and possessions. When Job persevered, Satan asked for permission to afflict him with disease. God also allowed this.

You will not be tested in areas too difficult for you. "There hath no temptation taken you but such as is common to man: but God *is* faithful, who will not suffer you to be tempted above that ye are able; but will with the temptation also make a way to escape, that ye may be able to bear *it*" (I Corinthians 10:13). The LORD also knows the feeling of temptation. Christ felt our temptations with us for He "… was in all points tempted like as we are, yet without sin" (Hebrews 4:15).

God does not tempt anyone, but He does permit it for the sake of strengthening the faith and endurance of believers. Satan daily petitions God to buffet and challenge God's elect. In Salvation, God placed on you the armor of Christ which perfectly protects you (Ephesians 6).

Glorify God in all things. Never be puffed up by your own accomplishments, for all you have is but a vaporous gift, given by God.

Diligently seek out your sins and confess them, for God is faithful and just to forgive them and cleanse you from all unrighteousness.

Answer *true* or *false*.

2.18 _____ God creates temptation.

2.19 _____ God promises a way to overcome all trials and temptation.

2.20 _____ God the Son has never known temptation.

2.21 _____ Satan is passive and simply waits for us to sin.

2.22 _____ Mature Christians have no weaknesses.

2.23 _____ The armor of God is something we must daily put on *ourselves*.

2.24 _____ God wants us to be conformed to the image of Jesus.

CHARACTER AND CONDUCT

John, Paul, and Peter all claim that Christians are to follow Christ's example for they are conformed into His likeness.

Wisdom and Knowledge. Isaiah speaks of the excellence of Christ in "...the spirit of wisdom and understanding, the spirit of counsel and might, the spirit of knowledge and of the fear of the LORD; and shall make him of quick understanding in the fear of the LORD: and he shall not judge after the sight of his eyes, neither reprove after the hearing of his ears: but with righteousness shall he judge the poor, and reprove with equity for the meek of the earth..." (Isaiah 11:2-4).

The source of all wisdom is God. When Daniel was confronted by the servants of Nebuchadnezzar to bring forth an interpretation of the king's dream, he sought God's wisdom. When his request was granted, his gratitude was expressed in praise and adoration. "Then was the secret revealed unto Daniel in a night vision. Then Daniel blessed the God of heaven... Blessed be the name of God for ever and ever: for wisdom and might are his... I thank thee, and praise thee, O thou God of my fathers, who hast given me wisdom and might, and hast made known unto me now what we desired of thee..." (Daniel 2:19-20, 23). Like Daniel, we must give God credit for all wisdom and knowledge.

Daniel was painfully honest and quick to give God public credit for his wonders. In his powerful public office, he lived an example to all those who saw him. He was known for his righteousness, conviction, honesty, and faithfulness to God and his friends. Even among the pagan influences of Babylon, he never abandoned his God nor his convictions.

Complete these statements.

2.25 The perfect example of wisdom and knowledge is _____ .

2.26 Daniel's reaction to God's giving him the dream interpretation was _____ .

2.27 Our abilities are a gift of God to bring _____ to God.

2.28 The characteristics received by Jesus from the Holy Spirit included a. _____ , b. _____ , c. _____ , d. _____ , e. _____ , and f. _____ . (Isaiah 11:2-4)

Answer this question.

2.29   How does Isaiah 11:2-4 indicate that the LORD's judgment will not be according to natural ability?

_____

_____

Moral purity. We are all pressured to sin, both within our hearts and from the fallen world. Our only standard of practice is the Bible, not the opinions of friends.

Study Scripture and act wisely. Set parameters for your behavior ahead of time according to God's word. This way, when a time of trial comes, there is no confusion or ambiguity. Where there is clarity, there is no choice.

Regulate your environment. Make friends that encourage your beliefs by holding you accountable and participate in righteous activities. We live and work in the world but we are not of the world.

Perhaps the hardest thing to control is your tongue. What you say and how you say it can either bless or curse. Your speech indicates that the Holy Spirit dwells in you, for out of the same mouth should not flow both good and bad. Our objective is to have Christ's character dominate our lives so that more and more of our conversation and speech are like the LORD's. Christ's speech encouraged, edified, and rebuked.

God's providence occasionally works against our desires and contradicts our commitments. For example, Paul promised the church at Corinth that he would try to make two visits to them. After this, he had to postpone his journey. The Corinthians believed that perhaps Paul's word could not be trusted. Therefore, do not make vows lightly, for we never know what God's tomorrow might bring. "For that ye *ought* to say, If the Lord will, we shall live, and do this, or that" (James 3:15). "... but let your yea be yea and *your* nay, nay; lest ye fall into condemnation" (James 5:12b).

Complete these statements.

2.30   The text for Christian faith and practice is _____ .

2.31   Set _____ for your behavior ahead of time.

2.32   Christians are not _____ the world.

2.33   Your speech should indicate that the Holy Spirit _____ .

2.34   Do not make _____ lightly.

2.35   God's _____ occasionally works against our desires.

SPIRITUAL DEVELOPMENT

Many people are committed to learning new facts or to improving their physical fitness. Nutrition and health foods have become a multibillion-dollar industry. Time spent jogging or exercising at health clubs is seen as a reasonable investment toward a better and a longer life. However, few people would be able to describe a similar commitment to their spiritual development.

Fellowship with God. If a young person had to choose between attending either an exegetical discourse on a meaty theological topic or attending a youth fellowship banquet, they probably would not have difficulty choosing. At the discourse they would meet older, wiser people who have a detailed knowledge of the Scripture texts. While at the banquet, they would meet young people who had come for food and entertainment. Unfortunately, most young people would choose the banquet.

True believers gather around God's Word for a banquet. We feast at God's banquet table when we hear His Word preached and take the Sacraments. True fellowship is found only through Christ. For the only fellowship we have with God is through Christ's mediation, as part of His Church (congregation of His of His elect). In a real way, fellowship with God is a corporate (rather than individual) activity.

The net result of true fellowship with God is our humble, joyful praise. "Make a joyful noise unto the LORD, all ye lands. Serve the LORD with gladness: come before his presence with singing... Enter into his gates with thanksgiving, *and* into his courts with praise: be thankful unto him, *and* bless his name" (Psalm 100:1-2, 4). "Praise ye the LORD. Sing unto the LORD a new song, *and* his praise in the congregation of saints... Let them praise his name in the dance: let them sing praises unto him with the timbrel and harp" (Psalm 149:1, 3).

God fellowships with us through Scripture. He unfolds His plan of salvation for His rebellious children and the depth of His love for us, sinners that we are. The Holy Spirit illumens the meaning from the passages of Scripture that you hear or read.

God the Holy Spirit is our Sanctifier. In Salvation we are given the Holy Spirit, and as we continue in this life, that same Person gradually makes us holy in the image of Christ. Although we will continue to sin until our deaths, the Spirit preserves us until the Judgement.

As Paul explained, our lives will continue to be marred by sins both intentional (commission: deliberately breaking God's Law) and unintentional (omission: failing to live up to the Law's requirements). But even unto the saved, God is righteous and just to forgive us our sins and cleanse us from all unrighteousness.

God demands holiness from those who seek to fellowship with Him. Thus, we are filled with the Spirit and declared holy. We are commanded to live like we are (Ephesians 5:18, 1 Peter 1:15).

God loves His people. They matter so much to Him that He sacrificed Himself for their benefit. If you are His, God will gradually make you spiritually mature. All you are or ever will be is in His hands.

Answer *true* **or** *false*.

2.36 _____ David's motivation for writing Psalms 100 and 149 was a desire to praise God.

2.37 _____ Bible reading and study is not a way of fellowship with God.

2.38 _____ Fellowship with God is an individual activity.

2.39 _____ We fellowship with God through hearing His Word and receiving the Sacraments.

2.40 _____ Quiet prayer is the only form of fellowship according to Psalm 100.

2.41 _____ The result of fellowship is humble, joyful praise.

2.42 _____ God fellowships with us through Scripture.

2.43 _____ The Holy Spirit makes us spiritually mature.

Match these items.

2.44 _____ sin of commission   a. work of the Holy Spirit

2.45 _____ man's worth is illustrated   b. God is righteous and just to forgive

2.46 _____ the Sanctifier   c. failure to fulfill the Law's requirements

2.47 _____ confession of sin   d. directly breaking God's Law

2.48 _____ sin of omission   e. Christ's death

Prayer. Prayer is the surest, most direct form of thanksgiving Christ's church has. We pray in order to confess our sins and thankfully acknowledge His mercies. Prayer is inspired by the Holy Spirit as communicated through (in the name of) Christ our mediator for the attention of our heavenly Father.

The five types of prayer are worship, thanksgiving, confession, petition, and intercession.

Worship and thanksgiving. "Hallowed be thy name, thy kingdom come, thy will be done on earth as it is in Heaven." Paul reminds us that we are to give thanks in everything, especially tragedy (1 Thessalonians 5:18). God our loving Savior is sovereign and all things happen together for His consummate glory.

Confession of sin. "Forgive us our debts..." Confession of sin is a daily activity of the repentant

BIBLE

LIFEPAC TEST

79

99

Name _____

Date _____

Score _____

BIBLE 1210: LIFEPAC TEST

Match these items (each answer, 2 points).

1. _____ especially needed during trials
2. _____ prayer for needs of others
3. _____ deliberately breaking God's Law
4. _____ the result of trials
5. _____ diverse and numerous
6. _____ failing to fulfill God's Law
7. _____ important in choosing a career
8. _____ leads to forgiveness
9. _____ Word preached and Sacraments received
10. _____ a request for your own needs

a. sin of commission
b. sin of omission
c. fellowship
d. spiritual growth
e. spiritual gifts
f. personality
g. petition
h. thanksgiving
i. intercession
j. confession

Answer *true* **or** *false* (each answer, 1 point).

11. _____ As you diligently study, the Holy Spirit guides you away from error.
12. _____ All people who call themselves Christians are Christians.
13. _____ The Holy Spirit dwells in church buildings just as God did in the Tabernacle.
14. _____ The Holy Spirit helps believers to discern truth.
15. _____ Jesus learned what God is like through the trials He endured.
16. _____ The Old Testament names ascribed to God were not applied to Jesus.
17. _____ God tempts us so that we can overcome it.
18. _____ Jesus will judge righteously according to what He sees and hears.
19. _____ The literature of a cult is important to apologetics.
20. _____ A pastor's occupation often becomes his family's identity.

Choose the correct answer (each answer, 2 points).

21. The Bible is the only book that reveals the _____ .
    a. sinfulness of man
    b. virgin birth of a man
    c. true nature of God
    d. Flood account

22. The historian Eusebius helped to determine the _____ .
    a. age of the earth
    b. downfall of Rome
    c. Pseudepigrapha
    d. New Testament canon

23. The King James Bible is properly called an english _____ .
    a. codex
    b. paraphrased edition
    c. original Bible
    d. version

24. God's goal for Christians is that they _____ .
    a. win the world for Christ
    b. conform to Jesus' image
    c. remain as children
    d. be tempted

25. One principle of the Christian faith is that Christians will produce _____ .
    a. a good income
    b. good children
    c. good crops
    d. good works

26. The primary motive in life for a Christian is to _____ .
   a. have a ministry
   c. establish a career
   b. glorify the LORD
   d. build a reputation
27. If a person wants to devote all of his time to pleasing the LORD, Paul said that he should not _____ .
   a. do secular work
   c. get married
   b. be tempted
   d. have children
28. Formally defending Christianity is called _____ .
   a. didactics
   c. dogmatics
   b. apologetics
   d. hermeneutics
29. If you are people oriented, all of these careers would be desirable except _____ .
   a. teaching
   c. truck gardening
   b. pastoring a church
   d. retail selling
30. Spiritual gifts are received _____ .
   a. through a ceremony
   c. from the Holy Spirit
   b. through prophecy
   d. by faith
31. The Old Testament name for God that implied the Trinity was _____ .
   a. Adonai
   c. Jehovah
   b. Elohim
   d. Messiah

Complete these statements (each answer, 3 points).

32. Christianity presents salvation obtained by a. _____ , and cults present salvation obtained by b. _____ .

33. Ephesians 4:23-32 describes the attribute of God's holiness as seen in _____ .

34. Unhappiness at home often results from a job that is _____ .

35. Jesus' redemptive work was completed on _____ .

36. A person is justified by _____ .

37. For the Christian the Bible is the rule of _____ .

38. To properly understand a Bible verse, you must read it _____ .

39. One of the most evident clues that the Holy Spirit dwells in a believer is his

   _____ .

Put these items in chronological order. These statements pertain to the experience of Israel (each answer, 2 points).

40. _____ God sought individual fellowship.
41. _____ YHWH was the God of Israel.
42. _____ God demands righteousness.
43. _____ God was known only as Creator.
44. _____ YHWH was seen as the one and only God.

2

Answer these questions (each answer, 5 points).

45.   What is the teaching of 1 Peter 3:15?

_____

_____

_____

46.   What can result from reading the same Bible verse over again?

_____

_____

_____

NOTES

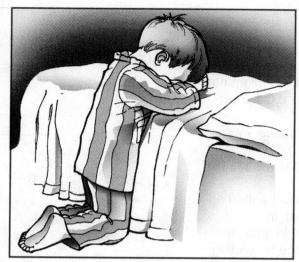

PRAYER IS OUR PRIMARY METHOD OF GIVING THANKS TO GOD.

Christian heart. Although our sins have been paid for, daily confession helps remind us of our own wretchedness and dependence on the perfect sweetness of the Gospel.

Petitions. "Give us this day our daily bread... lead us not into temptation, but deliver us from evil." God blesses His children with good things. Do not presume on His good graces nor ask for more than you need. To do so is arrogant presumption.

Intercession. "...as we forgive our debtors." Pray for the needs of all people, including enemies.

Choose the correct answer and write it on the line.

worship
thanksgiving
confession
presumption

petition
intercession
communication

2.49   God desires that we have constant _____ with Him.

2.50   A prayer given for your own needs is a _____ .

2.51   Joyful acknowledgement of God's goodness and provision is _____ .

2.52   Prayer is our primary method of _____ to God.

2.53   Prayers of _____ are a daily Christian activity.

2.54   We must offer prayers of _____ for the needs of others, especially our enemies.

2.55   Asking for what you don't need is arrogant _____ .

Scripture study. The Bible is the authoritative guide to faith and behavior. In order to grow spiritually, you must be familiar with God's Word. As you continue to study Scripture, the verses you memorize take on a deeper meaning. We will never have a complete understanding of all the depth of Scripture, but it is our duty to seek it out.

Find a method for disciplined study. Read some portion of Scripture every day, such as verses and chapters that have a common topic. Use a concordance or a chain reference Bible to identify verses. When you locate a verse, read the context both before and after the specific verse. This gives you a better impression of what the actual message is. As you read, take notes. Write questions as to things you do not quite understand. Write out new insights or truth. Note God's commands.

KEEP WORD IN MY HEART, NOT JUST HEAD!

GOD'S LAWS BRING ME JOY

✱ With my whole heart have I sought thee: O let me not wander from thy commandments. Thy word have I hid in mine heart, that I might not sin against thee. Blessed art thou, O LORD: teach me thy statutes.

⟶ I will delight myself in thy statutes: I will not forget thy word.

(Psalm 119:10-12, 16)

Let no man despise thy youth; but be thou an example of the believers, in word, in conversation, in charity, in spirit, in faith, in purity. Till I come, give attendance to reading, to exhortation, to doctrine. (1 Timothy 4:12-13)

OLD COVENANT OR NEW?

? TO EXHORT OR TO BE EXHORTED?

Through disciplined study, biblical doctrine will gradually be applied to your life. As you meditate on the Bible's content, the Holy Spirit will hide His Word in your heart. You yourself will be able to echo Psalm 119: 10-12, 16.

Answer *true or false.*

2.56 _____ A Bible verse can give new insight to each one who reads it.

2.57 _____ Spiritual growth can occur apart from God's Word.

2.58 _____ Specific passages of Scripture are not important to know.

2.59 _____ Knowing Bible texts stops you from sinning.

2.60 _____ Verses should be read in their larger context.

2.61 _____ Bible truth is too abstract and philosophical to help modern man.

2.62 _____ As long as you attend church, disciplined Bible study is unnecessary.

Answer this question.

2.63 What results from a repeat reading of the same Bible passages?

_____

_____

_____

Trials. Manifold tribulations come upon Christians as Satan attempts to cause them to stumble. However, trials often come because of pride, acting without wisdom, or having immature judgment. For example, overspending causes stress. Disabling illnesses or injuries sometimes result from imprudent action. After trials, Christians can more effectively pray for others in the same circumstances. Testing brings patience.

All trials are allowed by God. For example, even in captivity, Daniel was not rebellious or hateful, but

TRIALS ARE TO BE EXPECTED.

had a sincere concern for his captors. He continued to praise God for all that he was given. This thankfulness amidst tribulation strengthened his faith. He persevered. God allows trials in order to produce the fruit of correction, stronger faith, perseverance, and spiritual growth.

When trials are caused by sin, confession and repentance followed by humble thankfulness is the Christian's standard.

Our God is gracious. For when we sin, He is faithful and just to forgive us and cleanse us from all unrighteousness

---

✦ Choose the correct answer and write it on the line.

Satan   world
God   pride

2.64   Many of our problems are caused by our _____ .

2.65   Christians are targets of _____ .

2.66   Trials that come to Christians are allowed by _____ .

2.67   Although many trials come from the _____ , most are fostered by our sinfulness.

✦ Complete this activity.

2.68   List four benefits that God brings out of trials.

        a. _____

        b. _____

        c. _____

        d. _____

✦ Answer this question.

2.69   What is God's attitude toward Christians who sin? _____

        _____

        _____

        _____

✓ **Adult check** _____

                    Initial   **Date**

Review the material in this section in preparation for the Self Test. This Self Test will check your mastery of this particular section as well as your knowledge of the previous section.

Answer *true* or *false* (each answer, 1 point).

2.01 _____ The LORD expects us to use our spiritual gifts.

2.02 _____ The ability to know God is unrelated to God's gifts.

2.03 _____ God's goal for Christians is that they conform to the character and personality of Jesus.

2.04 _____ God creates temptation so that we can *overcome* it.

2.05 _____ Mature Christians have no weaknesses where Satan can tempt them.

2.06 _____ Jesus came to show man God's nature.

2.07 _____ The Holy Spirit does not dwell in church buildings.

2.08 _____ The best interpreter of the Word of God is the human heart.

2.09 _____ All Christians have the Holy Spirit dwelling in them.

2.010 _____ The names ascribed to God were not given to Jesus.

Choose the correct answer (each answer, 2 points).

2.011 The original language of the New Testament is _____ .
a. Hebrew   c. Greek
b. Roman   d. Aramaic

2.012 The *primary* original language of the Old Testament is _____ .
a. Hebrew   c. Chaldean
b. Egyptian   d. Greek

2.013 The historian who helped to determine the New Testament canon was _____ .
a. Tertullian   c. Eusebius
b. Diocletian   d. Clement

2.014 The one science that can greatly expand our knowledge of Bible times is _____ .
a. astronomy   c. dendrochronology
b. paleontology   d. archaeology

2.015 God cannot tolerate sin because He is _____ .
a. righteous   c. holy
b. loving   d. merciful

2.016 Spiritual gifts are received _____ .
a. by faith   c. through prophecy
b. by the laying on of hands   d. from the Holy Spirit

2.017 Jesus received all of these characteristics from the Spirit of God except _____ .
a. wisdom   c. might
b. deity   d. knowledge

2.018 Quiet prayer is a form of fellowship with God according to _____ .
a. Psalm 119   c. Psalm 100
b. Psalm 150   d. Psalm 23

2.019 Many of our problems are caused by _____ .
a. the world   c. pride
b. God   d. the Bible

2.020 David wrote Psalm 149 because he wanted to _____ .
a. complain to God   c. lead Israel
b. confess his sin   d. praise God

Complete these statements (each answer, 3 points).

2.021   The Bible is the only book that reveals the true nature of _____ .

2.022   God demands His people be holy because He is _____ .

2.023   To properly understand a Bible verse, you must read it in its _____ .

2.024   The text of faith and practice for a Christian is _____ .

2.025   Moral codes must be applied _____ .

2.026   We must especially thank God during times of _____ .

2.027   God cannot be tempted with evil, and He does not tempt _____ .

2.028   You evident that the Holy Spirit dwells in you through your _____ .

Match these items (each answer, 2 points).

2.029   _____   a request for your own needs

2.030   _____   hearing the Word, receiving the Sacraments

2.031   _____   leads to forgiveness

2.032   _____   important in career choice

2.033   _____   failing to live up to God's Law

2.034   _____   diverse and numerous

2.035   _____   the result of trials

2.036   _____   intentionally breaking God's Law

2.037   _____   prayer for other's needs, especially enemies

2.038   _____   should be given during trials

a. sin of omission
b. sin of commission
c. confession
d. thanksgiving
e. petition
f. intercession
g. personality traits
h. spiritual gifts
i. spiritual growth
j. fellowship

Answer these questions (each answer, 5 points).

2.039   What is justification by faith?

_____

_____

_____

2.040   According to Isaiah 11:2-4, how does Jesus judge?

_____

_____

2.041   What can result from reading the same Bible verses over again?

_____

_____

_____

2.042   What is God's attitude toward a Christian who sins?

_____

_____

_____

_____

2.043   What are spiritual gifts for?

_____

_____

III. CHRISTIANITY AND THE WORLD

As a Christian you are a member of the Kingdom of God. Every contact you make affects others' lives. You effect people through: (1) your vocation, (2) ministry, and (3) personal life.

SECTION OBJECTIVES

Review these objectives. When you have completed this section, you should be able to:

8. Identify the influences on vocational and ministry choices.

9. Explain the importance of proclaiming the Gospel.

VOCABULARY

Study these words to enhance your learning success in this section.

commission   flexibility

laymen

VOCATION

Most people work in the labor market. Each person's job or career has tremendous impact on their life. The nature of the work establishes a pattern for the entire life of a person's family. It determines economic standards, recreational patterns, and education demands.

Very few people today really enjoy or find fulfillment in their careers because they did not actively plan for it. They allow circumstances, financial pressures or family models to determine how they will spend their time. A job requires approximately (including transportation) ten hours per day and from five to six days per week. It determines your lifestyle and may control your outlook on life itself.

Many people hesitate to volunteer for church activities because their careers are so demanding. Many also resist because they try to avoid people. Christian service is to be performed out of thankfulness, not duty or resentment. Many do not know what talents they have, and therefore what role they can serve, while others are overtaxed without appropriate assistance, causing negativity and unhappiness at home.

ALL PEOPLE ARE CALLED TO A VOCATION.

All people are called to a vocation or occupation in this life, from mechanics to computer programmers and from ministers to presidents. Your vocation or calling can be discerned by what you like and what you are good at.

Complete this activity.

3.1   List the three areas in which you affect other's lives.

a. _____

b. _____

c. _____

Answer *true* **or** *false*.

3.2   _____   Your occupation is a personal choice affecting no one else.

3.3   _____   Most people dislike their work.

3.4	____	Everyone is called to be a minister.
3.5	____	Most people fail to adequately prepare to select a career.
3.6	____	The typical work week is twenty-five hours.
3.7	____	A ministry is occasionally a career.
3.8	____	People with careers cannot serve at their local church.
3.9	____	All pastors love their work.

Complete these statements.

3.10 A job that is over-demanding and causes unhappiness can also cause _____
_____

3.11 A vocation is _____

Career choice. Analyze your skills, what are you good at? How do you spend your free time outside of your school or job? Do you spend your time reading, being with people, working with tools, or gardening? What do you like doing? People tend to excel in areas for which they have sincere preference. If you are a "people"-oriented person, your preferences and skills are probably more developed in that area than with the "things" of a mechanically-oriented person. Similarly, if you really enjoy and excel in dealing with people, you would not be overly satisfied with a career that focuses primarily on ideas or data, theories or mathematics.

WHAT YOU ARE GOOD AT AND WHAT YOU LIKE DETERMINES YOUR CALLING.

The activities that you do for fun can be classified according to their relationship with ideas, people, or things. For instance, if you love to play basketball, for that sport may be a very people-oriented activity to you. You enjoy spending time with your friends, kidding around, and laughing with them. However, basketball to you may also

mean an opportunity to develop some very specialized techniques and skills. If you take a scientific approach to playing, then to you it is more idea oriented. You may simply like to be very physically active. You like to get the basketball in your hand, pound it against the floor, run down court with all your might, and force the ball to the hoop. This is manually, or things-oriented.

Complete these activities.

3.12 Think about the activities that you enjoy. Now, consider whether each activity is enjoyed because it relates more to ideas, people or things and mechanical operations. List each of your hobbies, pastimes, volunteer work, school subjects, or other activities according to its primary definition of being idea, people, or things oriented.

IDEAS OR DATA	PEOPLE	THINGS OR MECHANICAL

3.13 Review the three columns in 3.12. If there is a pattern showing where most of your preferences fall, enter the name of that column here: _____

3.14 Review your highest or top two highest preferences. List three jobs which you think would use these preferences the most.

a. _____
b. _____
c. _____

Adult check _____
                               Initial   **Date**

Determine what you value most in life. Your values are likely very different from the list of a nonchristian moralist or secularist. Fourteen common work values are:

achievement: performing well and reaching one's goals;

approval: having one's work rated favorably;

authority: the right to command or influence others;

conducive environment: having favorable surroundings;

contentment: feeling satisfaction with one's job;

creativity: being able to do original, imaginative things;

financial return: the amount of money received for working;

freedom: unrestricted self-determination;

harmony: experiencing agreeable relationships with others;

intellectual stimulation: arousing mental activity;

prestige: being held in high esteem by others;

security: the assurance of keeping one's job;

service: rendering assistance to others

variety: altering activities, avoiding routine.

Rank these in importance. Your rankings will likely change as your life changes. Right now, you may not feel any particular need for security. However, in ten years you may be married and have children, making job security an important factor. Remember, in the future, you may change and want to change your career accordingly.

Your motivations may also change. As a young person you may be motivated only to make enough money to pay for your automobile. You may even want to save for college. As an adult, your financial needs will be greater and your motivation may shift toward earning a greater salary. Think ahead. Plan where you would want to be in ten years. Visualize what your motivations will be.

If you have a job now, think through the reasons why you have begun working. Some work just for experience, while others work for the money. Young people also work for the opportunity to do good for others or just to kill time. As your life changes, remember your primary purpose in life is to glorify God and enjoy Him forever. Whatever your occupation, always consider your primary goal.

Be **flexible** and realistic in your career planning. Consider educational needs, work availability, and the nature of the work. If you prefer long terms of training, such as four to ten years of college, then the occupation you choose should be consistent with that preference. However, if you would like to enter the labor market as soon as you graduate from high school or after a short period of career preparation, then your career choice will be determined accordingly. Decide what your career will be before determining what kind of further education you will need. Take specified courses with specific application to your chosen profession.

The labor market dictates educational demands. As each year passes, a greater need exists for specifically trained technical workers with

TECHNICAL VOCATIONS MAY REQUIRE SPECIFIED TRAINING.

extensive computer skill. Near the middle of the 20th century, the average person had less than a high school education. Today, about 60 percent of all workers have at least some college or associates degree, and over 30 percent of all workers are college graduates. Jobs requiring little skill or ability have little to offer in flexibility, wages, career upward mobility, or freedom.

The widest range of availability is in the technical (computer-oriented), service-oriented, and supervisory-professional areas. These occupations usually require at least two years of vocational training and two or more years of specialized field training.

Your career may determine where you live, for some occupations are specialized to specific regions of the country. If you wish to be a missionary, you probably will work outside the United States. If you want to be a forest ranger, you will have to live near or within a forest. Petroleum engineers work with companies exploring for new oil finds. This work may mean living on an oil derrick twenty miles out over the ocean. Some military occupations take spouses away from their families for long periods of time. Consider what the job will demand of you in the working hours and lifestyle it will make

---

✎⊶ Complete these statements.

3.15   In the future, employers will expect more _____ .

3.16   Be a. _____ and b. _____ in your career planning.

3.17   The primary purpose of the Christian is to _____ .

3.18   In planning for a career, a person should picture his life _____ years ahead.

3.19   Unskilled jobs offer little opportunity for a. _____ , b. _____ ,
        c. _____ and d. _____ .

3.20   The highest demand for workers is now in a. _____ and b. _____ .

3.21   The nature of a career dictates much of the _____ of the family.

Some women work in occupations that do not require long-term career development, for they intend to work before marrying and having children. Others combine a career with family. When homemakers are in their mid-forties, some again look forward to working for wages. As a young adult, you may determine how effectively that transition is made. Continue to acquire skills and keep current throughout your homemaking years, so you can be confident to enter a job setting that you will enjoy. Any person who approaches the labor market as an unskilled worker, has little control over what kind of work they will perform.

Due to technological changes, some careers have disappeared altogether. Some careers are limited dramatically by Federal funding of projects where the jobs exist. For example, in the mid 1970s, space engineers were laid off by the tens of thousands due to NASA cutbacks. This kind of thing can happen to any profession, therefore flexibility is a must.

A career is a sequence of chosen occupations leading in a general direction to fulfilling the values of the worker using his God-given abilities. A career is more than a single job. If you had a career in a retail-sales industry as a salesperson and decided that you wanted to go on a salary rather than remain in a **commission** job, you might make a career step into management.

Managers sometimes decide that they are too confined by their responsibilities, so *they* change jobs. This type of move is often taken by those who find that they prefer a more hands-on people-oriented job, over one in supervision.

Occasionally, people change career fields altogether. This change often requires returning to school to gain some new skills. In other occasions, positions previously held could be used as an education equivalent. For instance, the man who was a retail salesperson and then became a manager could have the same type of responsibilities working in a hotel. In the hotel, his lifestyle and environment would be changed. This particular worker may have had to enroll in a management training program or at least a bookkeeping program for the hotel industry, but the change in occupation is made without a great deal of trauma or long term unemployment. However, most managerial positions require a B.A. or B.S. degree. This type of career change is rather common.

Complete this activity.

3.22   Interview a worker as they execute their duties. List ten of their job responsibilities. The worker can be yourself.

        a. _____
        b. _____
        c. _____
        d. _____
        e. _____
        f. _____
        g. _____
        h. _____
        i. _____
        j. _____

        Show the list to someone else and ask them for two other jobs where some of the same skills can be used.

        k. _____
        l. _____

MINISTRY

The Church. While some Christians are called into a full time paid ministry, all are called to some kind of work within their local churches.

The pastor and the professional staff of local churches are available to the congregation whenever they are needed. This demand on personal and family time must be seriously considered for anyone who is called to pastoral ministry, for the pastor's occupation often becomes the identity of the entire family. All of their recreational and personal activities are scheduled around the demands of the church or parish. For this reason, Paul suggested that men remain unmarried, because the demands upon a spiritual leader are tremendous.

The pastor's wife has a unique burden to bear. Unlike those whose husbands come home for dinner every day at a set time and have weekends and holidays off, a pastor's wife may seldom see her husband on a regular basis. Her children are "expected" to be perfect examples to the congregation and community. Her home must be available for visits by the congregation at almost any time. She may also be "expected" to teach or lead women's groups.

A Bible college education is typically the minimum requirement for ministers of the LORD. But after completing a four year degree, he is most likely to continue his training in a seminary.

Work within the Church is necessary for all God's children. Much work needs to be done by **laymen**, but few actually do it.

✐ **Complete these statements.**

3.23   One principle of the Christian faith is that Christians will produce _____ .

3.24   To avoid the demands that would take away time from ministering, Paul Suggested that a man _____ .

3.25   Every Christian is gifted by the LORD for work within the _____ .

3.26   The occupation of a pastor often becomes the family's _____ .

✐ **Complete this activity.**

3.27   Name one good work you can perform for the benefit of those outside the Church.

_____

_____

Teaching.   Everyone is a teacher, as we instruct our children, friends, co-workers, and others. We must study diligently in order to be apt for every opportunity. If you take the responsibility for preparing and conducting classes in your church, you must take it seriously and prepare for it.

Your first area of preparation is to know the Holy Scriptures. You will then want to learn time-proven teaching techniques that will supplement your natural ability. You will likely teach people younger than yourself. Therefore, study the unique characteristics of individual groups according to age, sex, occupation, and interests.

Many get experience as teachers and find that they excel. If you are sincerely interested in teaching, you may want to consider becoming a professional minister. Being a minister is the most challenging form of teaching, for you address a wide range of doctrine and shepherd the development of an entire congregation.

WE ARE ALL TEACHERS.

Evangelism. All Christians are required to understand the Gospel and be prepared to give a reason for their faith (1 Peter 3:15). Throughout our lives, we encounter people too numerous to count, who all need to be reconciled to their Holy Creator or face His wrath over their sin. However, many of these people are future members of the Kingdom of God. The Gospel itself is the power of God unto Salvation, which is why we evangelize (proclaim the Gospel). Faith is produced by the Holy Spirit through the hearing of the Gospel.

In the beginning, God created all that exists, making all things good. As His crowning achievement, He created mankind to bear His image in holiness as His lieutenant to rule and care for His earth. However, mankind abandoned its happy, joyful covenant with his Maker through an act of cosmic treason (eating the fruit of knowledge) because he wanted to be his own god. In committing this sin, Adam doomed himself and his posterity to separation from God, for His holiness cannot commune with sin. The human race justly deserved to be destroyed like the dust they are for breaking the covenant, but God loved rebellious mankind so much that He was gracious enough to plan (before Creation) a reconciliation of a remnant of them back to Himself.

God sent His Law, prophets, and teachers to announce this gracious reconciliation through substitutionary atonement (something else receiving the punishment deserved by you). However, in response man ignored His Laws and murdered His prophets, only compounding His guilt. To fulfill His plan, He Himself (Jesus Christ) condescended to come among his creatures to show them the only way back to Himself. They murdered Him. Through their evil act, He accepted the just punishment due to all of God's children upon Himself (the Crucifixion). Through their murderous act, God reconciled all those who but believe back to Himself (the Atonement), thus reversing for them the death brought by Adam's rebellion. Believers though born children of Adam, are instead children of Christ (Adoption) who will live forever with Him, the way life that was intended to be at the time of Creation.

The need of humanity is not self-esteem or happiness, it is redemption from God's wrath. Proclaim this Gospel in the earth and remember it well yourself. It is the power of God, and the only way to have access to Him.

CHRISTIANS ARE REQUIRED TO UNDERSTAND THE GOSPEL AND DECLARE IT TO OTHERS.

Complete these activities.

3.28   Memorize 1 Peter 3:15 and write the verse here. _____

_____

_____

_____

3.29   Write out the Gospel as you would proclaim it in evangelism. Next, write it out as you would proclaim it in order to re-inspire a backslidden Christian. Limit each to one page in length.

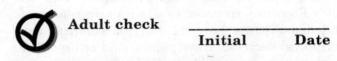

Adult check _____

                            Initial   Date

Apologetics. Apologetics is the defense of the Christian faith against heretics or purveyors of false doctrine. A Christian must be informed and able to skillfully debate on points of doctrine and error. Some occasions like this become opportunities for evangelism. However, if a person's heart is not softened by the truth of the Gospel, a debate at least gives others who are listening the truth, possibly preventing them from falling into heresy themselves.

Apologetics are defined as either *general* or *specialized*. Generalized apologetics is the ability to clearly explain basic Christian doctrine. You must know proof texts from the Scriptures to identify the sources of your belief, thereby explaining why you believe what you believe. This is absolutely critical. Many people choose to go to classical Bible colleges for the first years of their college education to strengthen their Christian foundation.

Besides knowing basic Christian doctrine, you should understand various denominational interpretations of certain passages. These interpretations result in the various types of worship and teaching distinct to each denomination. These are typically minor, secondary variations not directly having to do with the Gospel. For example, differing opinion arose among the writers of the New Testament books. Paul once said that men should not marry due to the split responsibilities between God and a household (1 Cor 7:32-33). However, Peter was married. These minor practical differences do not imply error nor heresy.

Clearly understand Church history in order to discern which teachings are a matter of tradition, custom, or preference. In your church, the custom may be to kneel when you pray. Because the Scriptures do not require a particular prayer position, other churches will justifiably differ in their customs. However, if the Scriptures are clear, then it is a doctrinal matter which must be understood and documented with Scriptural references.

Many of those who know little about Church history think that hundreds of different Christian religions exist because of the different names and customs used. However, the differences arise from Church history. For example, the German Church approaches the practice of their religion differently than does the Greek Church. Some support quiet, reserved worship, while others welcome robust singing and hand clapping. The common denominator of all is Jesus Christ's redemptive death and physical Resurrection. Therefore, a common bond exists among all Christians. Practices and traditions, without distorting these central truths, simply makes Christianity more understandable to a wide variety of people.

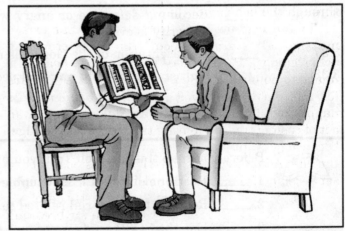

PRACTICE APOLOGETICS WITH OTHER CHRISTIANS.

Specialized apologetics focuses on the specific errors and heresies of individual cults. To do this, you must read comparative literature by the Christians who have gone before and studied the cult. Seek out expert sources to verify your material.

After you have studied the doctrinal errors, practice defending the truth with another Christian who has a similar level of understanding of the cult's practices. Role play the position of a cult member or apologist. Practice responding to specific challenges against Christian doctrine. Determine what approach you would take if someone asked you to prove that the Bible is the Word of God or that Jesus Christ lived and died and rose again.

You should be thoroughly familiar with the cult's literature in order to cite its own references and demonstrate how its doctrine conflicts with Scriptural doctrine. Have your friend critique you. Evaluate your approach, avoid becoming defensive or angry. Use good reasoning and God's wisdom.

When you deal in these areas, be continuously in prayer to protect you from falling into error yourself. John warned his friends not to allow the cultists of his day into their homes, for the Gnostics had taken on some of Christianity's characteristics (2 John 1:10-11). Remember that most modern cultists are highly moral people, but they are still under God's wrath.

After a clear defense of the truth, it is often time to present the Gospel in it's entirety. Typically, cult followers are good-intentioned people that have been deceived by their leaders. A simple presentation of their total depravity and Christ's atoning sacrifice may (by God's grace) win them into His Kingdom.

Complete these statements.

3.30   Apologetics is a defense of the _____ faith.

3.31   One of the Apostles who was married was _____ .

3.32   Differences arise among churches because of _____ .

3.33   The common denominator among all Christians is Christ's a. _____ and
b. _____ .

Answer *true* **or** *false*.

3.34   _____ Specialized apologetics necessitates becoming familiar with the doctrine of a particular cult.

3.35   _____ To adequately defend Christianity against a cult, you must be thoroughly familiar with the literature of the cult.

3.36   _____ Becoming defensive or angry when defending the faith is acceptable because your sincerity is evident.

3.37   _____ A presentation of the Gospel is not necessary when you are defending the faith.

3.38   _____ Cultists are usually immoral people.

Before you take this last Self Test, you may want to do one or more of these self checks.

1. _____ Read the objectives. Determine if you can do them.

2. _____ Restudy the material related to any objectives that you cannot do.

3. _____ Use the SQ3R study procedure to review the material:
a. **S**can the sections.
b. **Q**uestion yourself again (review the questions you wrote initially).
c. **R**ead to answer your questions.
d. **R**ecite the answers to yourself.
e. **R**eview areas you didn't understand.

4. _____ Review all activities and Self Tests, writing a correct answer for each wrong answer.

Choose the correct answer (each answer, 2 points).

3.01   In the future, employers will expect from their employees more _____ .
    a. work   c. time
    b. education   d. loyalty

3.02   The primary motivation in life for a Christian is to _____ .
    a. build a reputation   c. glorify the LORD
    b. establish a career   d. have a ministry

3.03   One principle of the Christian faith is that Christians will produce _____ .
    a. children   c. an adequate income
    b. good works   d. their own food

3.04   Formally defending Christianity is called _____ .
    a. dogmatics   c. scholastics
    b. hermeneutics   d. apologetics

3.05   A modern translation of the Bible is a New International _____ .
    a. Corruption   c. Version
    b. Interpretation   d. Translation

3.06   The science that can expand our knowledge of Biblical languages is _____ .
    a. morphophonemics   c. phonology
    b. linguistics   d. astrology

3.07   The Roman emperor who tried to destroy the Scriptures was _____ .
    a. Eusebius   c. Julius
    b. Augustus   d. Diocletian

3.08   To properly understand a Bible verse, you must read it _____ .
    a. quickly   c. in its context
    b. in English   d. after prayer

3.09   One of the most evident clues that the Holy Spirit dwells in you is your _____ .
    a. smile   c. clothing style
    b. speech   d. church denomination

3.010   Quiet prayer is a form of fellowship according to _____ .
    a. Psalm 100   c. Paul
    b. Tertullian   d. II John

Match these items (each answer, 2 points).

a. ideas
b. people
c. things

3.011   _____ go shopping with a friend
3.012   _____ fix your own lamp
3.013   _____ work in the garden
3.014   _____ read the Bible
3.015   _____ teach Sunday school
3.016   _____ play with children
3.017   _____ discuss theology

Answer *true* **or** *false* (each answer, 1 point).

3.018	_____	The literature of a cult is not important when discussing Christianity with a cult member.
3.019	_____	The presentation of the Gospel is not important when defending Christianity against a cult.
3.020	_____	The occupation of a pastor often becomes the family's identity.
3.021	_____	Every Christian is gifted by God to do some work within the Church.
3.022	_____	Most people fail to adequately prepare to select a career.
3.023	_____	The Bible is the only book that reveals the true nature of the Trinity.
3.024	_____	All Christians have the Holy Spirit dwelling in them.
3.025	_____	The name Yahweh suggests the characteristic of God as Father.
3.026	_____	God does not allow temptation to come to His children.
3.027	_____	David wrote Psalm 149 as a praise to God.
3.028	_____	God's goal for Christians is that they conform to the character and personality of Jesus.

Complete these statements (each answer, 3 points).

3.029 Paul said that a man desiring to devote his time exclusively to the LORD should avoid _____ .

3.030 The common denominator among all Christians is Christ's a. _____ and b. _____ .

3.031 A vocation is an _____ .

3.032 God cannot tolerate sin because He is _____ .

3.033 The original languages of the Old Testament were _____ .

3.034 In the Old Testament the word for God that suggested the Trinity was _____ .

3.035 The verses in Ephesians 4:23-32 describe in the life of the believer the result of God's attribute of _____ .

3.036 The only rule of faith and practice for the Christian is _____ .

3.037 Prayer on behalf of the needs of others is _____ .

3.038 Failing to live up to God's Law is a sin of _____ .

3.039 _____ is vital to all prayer, especially during trials.

Answer these questions (each answer, 5 points).

3.040 What is the primary difference between Christianity and a cult concerning justification?

_____

_____

3.041 What is the primary purpose of spiritual gifts?

_____

_____

3.042 What is the teaching of 1 Peter 3:15?

_____

_____

_____

What is the result of an occupation that is over-demanding?

_____

_____

_____

81/101

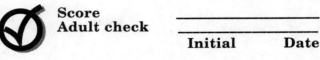

Score
Adult check _____

Initial   Date

Before you take the LIFEPAC Test, you may want to do one or more of these self checks.

1. ____ Read the objectives. Determine if you can do them.

2. ____ Restudy the material related to any objectives that you cannot do.

3. ____ Use the SQ3R study procedure to review the material.

4. ____ Review all activities and Self Tests, and LIFEPAC Glossary.

5. ____ Restudy areas of weakness indicated by the last Self Test.

GLOSSARY

canon. The content of our present Bible consisting of sixty-six books; formally ratified by the council at Carthage in A.D. 397.

commission. Payment to an employee on the basis of a percent of the money received for either services or the sale of goods and products.

condescension. The act of leaving a high position or status and taking on a lowly, self-denying or common position.

flexibility. Having the ability to be changed or altered.

herald. Messenger, standard-bearer.

laymen. Church members not on salary by the church or a Christian organization; individual members.

linguistics. The scientific study of language in its present or ancient form.

metaphysical. The study of God and His range of functioning throughout the universe and throughout time.

polytheism. The belief in multiple gods.

NOTES